Dr. Lee,

thank you for your kindness, generosity, care, compassion, and love over the years for Dr. Gary and I.

You and your staff have helped my body and mind Heal over the years. Many of these poems were inspired through that Healing process.

May these poems, memories and photos fill your Heart with joy and Hope. May you Be inspired to share these words with others to Bring Hope.

What People Are Saying About
New Day Inspirations: A Poetry Journey

Rebecca Strobl shares her poetic artistry to blaze an activating message for reflection, perspective, and inspiration. This is a book one can't read without being moved to fuel the improvement we all want in our lives. Thank you, Rebecca for the challenge and doing it in a way the hits softly but moves us profoundly and immediately. The book is purposeful poetry for life.

—Bruce Pulver, Author of *Above the Chatter, Our Words Matter: Powerful Words that Changed My World Forever*

Rebecca is a very kind soul, always helpful, always there, she gives to others with the greatest of care! She takes us on a life journey with a tapestry of emotions and experiences, giving us hope and renewed proveniences! Giving us a beacon of hope and inspiration, she connects our hearts and minds, with POETRY of creative motivation!
This book is an inspirational journey that will lift your SPIRITS, in the end, it has no limits!

—Charles "Chuck" Andrews, CPP
Founder & COB - Friends of Chuck (FOC), Author of *Y.E.S. SIR*

New Day Inspirations: A poetry journey is a rare gem and precious gift I didn't know I needed. Rebecca's infectious smile and positive outlook continue to permeate throughout this book as she invites us along on her personal yet inspirational journey of love, hope, and faith. A must-read!

—Wanda Dunham, MPA, Retired Police Chief, author of *Becoming Chief, LIfe Lessons Learned On The Road Less Traveled*

New Day Inspirations: A Poetry Journey is like reading a letter from a friend with the words of comfort, encouragement and hope that lift you up when life has knocked you down. Rebecca's heart for others shines through in this book.

—Emily Crawford

New Day Inspirations

A Poetry Journey

New Day Inspirations

A Poetry Journey

Rebecca Strobl, CPP, EMT-I

NEW DAY
Education & Motivation

New Day Inspirations: A Poetry Journey
©2024 Rebecca Strobl

Published by Carpenter's Son Publishing, Franklin, Tennessee

Cover photograph by Rebecca Strobl

All photos within the book from the Rebecca Strobl Archives

Professional author photo, back cover and inside the book: Bobbi Jo Photography

Edited by Anne Tatlock

Cover and Interior Design by Suzanne Lawing

Printed in the United States of America

978-1-956370-71-3

Dedication

This book is dedicated to my Savior and eternal best friend whose miraculous work in my life has inspired many of these poems. HE fills my heart with hope and joy when I need it the most.

My husband, Dr. Gary Strobl, whose love, support, and encouragement over the decades have inspired me to achieve things I never dreamed possible.

My sister who, when I started writing these poems, encouraged me to continue and believed I would be a published author in my adult life.

My fire and emergency services colleague, Chief Eddie Robinson, whose enthusiastic support of my volunteer leadership fire and emergency services path fanned the flames of my service to my community and beyond in a capacity I never imagined as a youth when I wrote many of these poems.

My virtual assistant, Emily Crawford, of Hey Emily, who carefully transferred these poems from the paper where they had lived for decades into the digital document that became this book.

My literary coach, Tiarra Tompkins, of The Legacy Architect, whose knowledge of taking raw documents and transforming them into manuscripts ready for publication is outstanding.

My security and fire family whose respect, support, and commitment to their industries have inspired me to be a better professional. It is an honor to mend our broken world together.

My closest friends, whose continuous presence in celebrating my successes and sharing words of encouragement during times of struggle have been more precious to me than gold.

My previous poem recipients, who provided me feedback when I wrote them personal poems to encourage them during their journey. Your feedback was appreciated and fueled my desire to share my writing with the world.

Hello Reader,

You are about to embark on an incredible journey, one that will take you through a myriad of experiences, emotions, and memories. These poems reflect portions of my life and often my faith that continues to guide me. I have considered sharing these thoughts with you for many years, though it never seemed like the right time. I am thrilled to present them to you now. As you join me in this poetry journey, you may find our faiths and life experiences look very different. These differences provide us with an amazing opportunity to learn from each other.

It is my sincerest desire as you read these poems, stories, and inspirational insights that you are encouraged to believe hope is not lost. It is my prayer that you will see the possibility of hope being restored within the pages of this book. This book was written to include not only faith-based poems that strengthened me on my journey, but also poems I have written to encourage others. No matter what your life journey looks like, I hope you will find the HOPE and care that has been carefully woven throughout each page.

This book is more than just a collection of poems and stories. It is a resource of inspiration that you can come return to frequently to find hope and inspiration as you boldly walk into your destiny.

~ Rebecca Strobl, CPP, EMT-I

Themes

Introduction

Life is a series of moments. Like a heartbeat, those moments go up and down, taking us to the highest peaks and the lowest valleys. All too often, we face moments (both good and bad) when we struggle to find the words to express our feelings. What happens when we hit a mental block while seeking to provide the words, the encouragement to help ourselves or others?

This was my experience when I wrote my first poem at 17 years old during a mission trip to Eden, Jamaica. Our team of 30 teenagers and four leaders was there to construct a water tank for a deaf school. I found myself far from home, in a strange place, struggling physically to continue the challenging work of building a water tank in a tropical climate. There was an extremely low point during those two months when exhaustion, sickness, and loneliness rocked me to the core. I prayed for healing and comfort to continue doing my part to bring clean water to the people of Jamaica. It was at that moment the words of my first poem were written. After that trip, I continued writing poetry and made an amazing discovery. The poems I wrote put words to the feelings I struggled to unpack and provided me with the hope to push through even the hardest of times.

Instead of listening to the voices that sought to hold me back, I made the commitment to help myself and others turn struggles into strengths. To be the enthusiastic voice of hope, knowledge, and motivation in the lives of others.

Poetry became a beacon of light in putting my commitment into action. It quickly became an amazing resource in sharing insights and inspiration with others. Words flowed freely in cards, letters, and emails to others during key life moments. A simple gift received in a time of despair became a way to come alongside others on their journey with understanding and friendship.

Throughout my career, I have had the opportunity to work in sales, security, emergency medical services, and even as the first female fire chief in the Lake Arrowhead (Georgia) Volunteer Fire Department's and Cherokee County's (Georgia) history. Each of these opportunities gave me new experiences and helped me see things differently. The more incredible experiences I had and people I met, the more the poetry flowed from my pen.

It is no accident that you are holding this book today. Contained within these pages are experiences, lessons, and personal stories to inspire you. Each poem, photo, and story is an original work, collected and put together in one place to awaken the power of creativity in you. Each of us has an incredible and unique footprint to create in this world. As you prepare to join me on this journey, let the words and experiences encourage you to pursue your passions. I will be with you all along the way, walking beside you, encouraging you to conquer your mountains and showing you that you are so capable of accomplishing extraordinary things.

I pray that as you flip through these pages you can find hope and perhaps a different perspective to this life. May these poems brighten your time traveling life's journey. Let's go on an inspirational journey together!

Nature

World

The sky is a deep blue
But God does love you true and true.
The birds sing loud and clear
But our Heavenly Father is always to His children so very near.
The grass is a gorgeous green
But Christ is always someone on whom we can lean.
Nature is a wondrous sight
But Christ is always ready to hold onto us tight!

Memories

Where do you feel at home?

Is it in a big bright city? Or maybe you are like me, and you love being outdoors. See, I grew up on a dirt road in an old farmhouse. We had an acre of land in Michigan that was surrounded on three sides by a farmer's fields. At the rear of our property between us and one of those fields was a mini forest. I can remember during those formative years that I loved sitting in that mini forest with the trees or if I was feeling even more adventurous, I would ride my bike several miles down the dirt road and visit the park.

I felt closer to God when I spent time outdoors and found it a great place to meditate on my blessings, reflect and pray about whatever challenge I was facing at that point in my life, and truly get back to the basics and simplicity that life can hold for us.

My love of nature followed me into adulthood and now, two of my favorite places to walk are in the community where Gary and I live in the North Georgia mountains, and a campground in a national forest in North Georgia. The creative side of my brain still soars when I am outdoors and breathing deeply, just like it did when I was a child out in nature. I hope this poem inspires you to unplug for a few moments (no looking at your phone), get outside, slow down, and reflect on what you do have in your life instead of thinking about what you may lack.

Peaceful Night

Sleeping under the stars
My mind wanders far
Who has made the stars I see
And does HE know about me?
The moon peeks around its dark cloak
Looking for a shadow to invoke
The compositions of crickets fill the peaceful night
Displaying their melodious might.
The sun quietly sleeps
While the moon radiates from the deep.
Fireflies illuminate their light
Giving weary travelers light.
The peaceful night brings rest to a weary soul
Upon whom life has taken its toll.
Popping, cracking, burning pine
Provides warmth and sweet air while the traveler dines.
His weary body finds a satisfying bed of soft grass
After enjoying fire roasted bass.
Life slows down to a quiet hum
Making the pains of progress numb.
I lay upon my soft bed
And am thankful I am well fed.
The splendor of creation
Overwhelms my heart on this special occasion.
My heart has found peace in this night
Driving out all my paralyzing frights.
I have met the Creator of the sparkling sky
And I have hope when I die.

Inspiration

What do you see when you stare into the night sky?

There truly is nothing that can compare to gazing at the night sky filled with sparkling stars. It must be why I love camping so much. One night, while I was thinking about the beauty I saw in the evening sky, I wrote this poem that speaks of my belief in the ONE who created nature's beauty.

Lakes

When I gaze at your body you do shake
From the wind's strong hand, you do quake.
Your waters seem mighty and rough
But the ONE who made you did not find HIS task rough.
HIS awesome hand skillfully formed you
So you could be your ocean blue.

Inspiration

This photo always takes me back to my honeymoon. Gary, my husband, snapped this shot as I looked over Lake Michigan. In that moment, I was thinking about my times as a youth on the shores of Lake Huron. My family would take our camper to a campground at the lake during the summer when my sister and I were out of school. I loved to sit on the beach for hours and watch the waves, feel the wind on my face, listen to the waves crash onto the shore, listen to sea gulls communicate with each other, and watch the water turn different shades of blue based on the clouds above.

My favorite time to be on shore and around the lake was when there were storms many miles out on the lake and the waves would become very big and choppy. The winds would howl as they blew across the lake. I marveled at the power of the waves and wind. Early on I saw a similarity between these storms of nature and the struggles and storms of our own lives. Challenges can seem to arise suddenly, but even amid the unexpected stress, we can remain calm and hopeful. That hope is the key to calm in the storm.

The Marsh

The fog wrapped marsh awakes from its misty dream
While its waters dazzle in the morning sun's beams.
Ducks and loons converse in their fowl tongue
Ensuring their song is sung.
The hills rise with elegance and grace
Giving the remote marsh a majestic face.
Feisty fish jump out of the water
Seeking an escape from their approaching slaughter.
The fishing lines are cast.
Will it be famine or feast?
The reeds sway with the gentle breeze
As our boat drifts with the gentle breeze.
Over the hills the sun begins to rise
Becoming smaller and smaller in size.
Our faces relish the warm light
And inspire us for our fish fight.
A jerk, a pull, the line is alive.
An angry pike with the line takes a dive.
The rod bends with the fighting weight
As the champion of the water swims at an alarming rate.
Frantically reeling has brought the hefty fish in sight.
He dives beneath the boat with all his might.
The mighty fisherwoman has finally won
For she holds the prize fighter's fin.
With new zeal and excitement, she lets out her line
Asking herself, "What other fish will be mine?"
The warm sun, steady breeze and fresh air
All remind her she is in a place so rare.
You can find without casting a ton
That life is simple fun, and you can soak up the sun.

Memories

Do you enjoy fishing? Some of us grow up with fond memories of fishing with our families and the rest of us may have some outlandish story that kept us from the water for years.

As a kid, I would see my father leave to go fishing with his friend, often returning home with fish he caught that he turned into delicious fish dinners. It made me want to learn to fish. Unfortunately, my time fishing was very short as a child.

It all started with a rubber raft. See, my father had given me limited instructions on how to use a fishing rod and reel. Still, I thought I knew what I was doing the first time he finally took me fishing. Early into our time in the boat on the water, I cast out the fishing line with the hook attached to it and immediately felt like I had landed the big one. What I hooked was not a big fish, but the boat. I immediately found out the hard way that children, sharp hooks, and a rubber boat do not mix.

We sprung a leak and had to paddle super-fast to get back to the boat dock before everything that was in the boat sank to the bottom of the lake. No more fishing for me. After that, my interest in fishing was nonexistent. I figured I had shown myself, and everyone with me that day, that I wasn't meant to be fishing.

It just so happened that many years later when I met and married Gary, he wanted us to go fishing together. That was one of his favorite hobbies. He had done it with his family since he was very young. One of the places his family fished together was a camp in Canada in the Ontario province. I brought up the near sinking of our family's rubber boat and how I might not be the best fishing buddy. Gary assured me they did not use rubber raft boats in Canada. Before we ever left for our trip, he began to teach me how to use a bait casting rod in our driveway by having me cast a lure at buckets. This time when I used my newly acquired skills in the boat in Canada, I hooked fish and not the boat.

The marsh was beautiful, and the fish tasted delicious for dinner. The beauty of the marsh stood out to me, and I wanted to capture it the best way I could. This time also helped me learn a valuable lesson. Do not be afraid to go after skills you thought previously were not for you. Sometimes, we just need the right mentor to guide us in successfully accomplishing the task or learning the skill.

Roses

Roses are red
Violets are blue
God does love you
True and true

Inspiration

Flowers of all kinds can bring so much joy and beauty to our lives. This brief rendition of the traditional "Roses are red" came to my mind when I was gazing at the beautiful roses and thinking about the beauty of God's love for us.

How can you bring love's beauty into someone's life today?

Creation

The waves shout God's praise
Using their tides to proclaim God's praise.
The trees wave their leaves, branches exalting God's name
So HE can receive all the fame.
Creation sings of God's glory
So mankind can know the salvation story!

Inspiration

I have marveled often at the sights before me and reflected on God's power to create such amazing beauty. There are so many beautiful sights that I have been blessed to see throughout my life. Let's choose each day to find beauty and see the miracles that abound in our world.

Ducks, Birds, Dogs

Ducks quack
God will never be in lack.
Birds sing
God will make your heart to sing.
Dogs pant
God does not know the word can't!

Inspiration

Did you ever find yourself at the park, pondering the mysteries of life while feeding the ducks? Seeing and hearing ducks outdoors when I was a teenager brought me so much joy. This poem was written to encourage our faith in the God who provides for us and our hearts to sing out of gratitude.

What things can you express gratitude for in your life?

Family

Sisters

We can jam
And give Newsboys music a slam.
We know how to get down
And take away our frowns.
We do the above to praise the Lord.
Doing this we are never bored.
To each other we are good listeners.
We are sisters!

Memories

Family memories can hold some of the most profound joy and open your eyes to things you didn't even know to dream.

This poem was written after my sister and I took a road trip along the coast of Lake Huron. We had a fun time exploring new places together and talking about our life plans. She was in high school, and I was beginning my college journey. When we got home, I shared the poem I had written about our trip. She loved it! She thought it was a neat way to remember our trip beyond just the photos.

Over the next year I shared with her my new poems and each article I wrote for the community college's newspaper. During this time before transferring from the community college I had been attending to Oral Roberts University in Oklahoma, my sister gave me a very special gift. She gave me a framed photo of a typewriter and wrote a note encouraging me to become a published author.

Her belief in me as a published author helped keep my dream alive. Her gift to me of a typewriter photo is one of the reasons you are reading this poem today. What is your dream? What picture captures that dream? What picture and customized note can you share with a friend to encourage them in pursuit of their dream?

Children

Children are a precious gift.
They do bring an unchangeable shift.
They are a special blessing
And the ONE who made them is easy in addressing.
They make us smile
And for them we will go the extra mile.
Their sweet laughter fills our hearts with joy from the start.
HIS name is one of love.
HE did come from above.
God is the One
That loves these precious ones a ton!

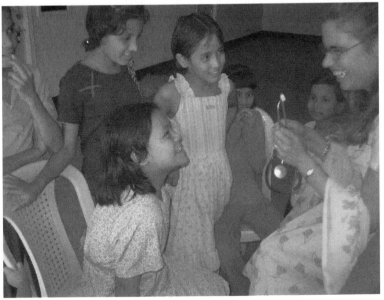

Inspiration

So many people in our lives will leave an imprint. For me, I have experienced the positive impact of a few adults believing in me and showing me God's love during my childhood. In my teenage years, I worked with at-risk youth in America and during international mission trips. That gave me a front-row seat to witness the great void that is created when children are not valued.

I have further witnessed that supporting children while they learn about various career paths can be the spark in helping them do amazing things. This poem was written to remind you of the gift each child's life represents and inspire you to show kindness to each one you meet.

Marry

When 2 people want to marry
They both must carry
A special kind of love
That only comes from above.
So as you two approach the altar
Remember not to falter
In your faith in God!

Inspiration

This poem was written to share with couples I knew who were getting married. I thought in the future when I published my poetry, it would be nice for people of faith to have a quick poem to share with friends they knew who were getting married. You never know what kind of hope you can share or instill in others until you share words meant to do simply that!

Careers

Leaders

Leaders are forged in life's most challenging fires
Often in the pursuit of helping others set
aside their personal desires,
Compassion and courage shine as their currency
When called upon to serve their communities in times of urgency,
They tackle life's challenges with professionalism and calm
So others can be inspired in life's storms to choose calm,
They clothe themselves with humility and honor
And become the true heroes of the hour,
They often risk their own lives
So others can survive and thrive,
They motivate and equip others to exceed their abilities
So these individuals can fully realize their amazing capabilities,
They never seek greatness or glory
and let the goodness they generate to those
around them be their story,
Choose to be this leader every day,
And help others experience their New Day!

Memories

The journey of leadership is not an instant one. It is composed of moments in which we have a choice to use our talents to meet a need and make a positive difference or stay in the shadows wishing for change. My path to leadership from a professional perspective started when I was a teenager. I can remember having a need to fund some of my own living and transportation expenses. So, at 16, I started my first job as a cashier at McDonald's.

I worked hard to learn the ropes quickly, provide excellent customer service to my clients, and learn valuable leadership lessons from my managers. I remained faithful in that role throughout high school and while I attended the local community college before transferring to Oral Roberts University (ORU) in Tulsa, Oklahoma. My efforts were recognized by the store manager after I graduated high school and started at the community college. She offered to send me through Hamburger University so I could become a supervisor and ultimately a store manager.

My focus was on transferring to ORU and becoming a medical missionary, so when this opportunity for additional leadership training dropped in my lap, I was reluctant to fully commit. When I first started at McDonald's, I was nervous. The thought that I might be able to make learning the ropes of being a McDonald's cashier and giving excellent customer service a FUN experience jumped out at me. So I said yes to the first level of leadership training at Hamburger

University. This meant I would become a new hire trainer and a mentor to new employees.

My job turned into a calling, making new employees feel welcome and well equipped to perform their job. Our employee retention rates improved dramatically, and it was not easy saying goodbye to my McDonald's team when I transferred to ORU.

FIRST LEADERSHIP LESSON: it is not about you, but about improving others' lives.

The next lesson came when I had to step away from continuing my college education at Oral Roberts University because the limited funds that started me at ORU as a transfer student were gone. I took a job as a front desk agent at a Sheraton Hotel in Tulsa whose main clientele was business travelers Sunday through Thursday and sports teams or conference attendees Friday and Saturday.

I enjoyed interacting with our guests, de-escalating stressful situations when their experience was not 100% satisfactory, finding creative ways to reduce the learning curve for new team members, celebrating my colleagues' strengths, and working additional shifts when the hotel was at full occupancy. The general manager noticed these efforts and promoted me to the position of front desk trainer / lead supporting the manager.

Once again, I was faced with an opportunity to accept a role in leadership and become the change I wanted to see at the hotel. The manager started giving me more opportunities to handle our schedules, new hire training, and improving communication between all departments of the hotel. We started feeling like a family at the hotel instead of simply employees all thrown together at a physical location. I loved the role and my team.

SECOND LEADERSHIP LESSON: Turn what seems like a setback into an opportunity to make a difference in a new way. Look through others' eyes to understand why they appear to be failing as a leader and see how you can lighten their load for the wellbeing of the organization.

Life is ever changing, and it wasn't going to stop now. Thanks to my job at the hotel funding my living and educational expenses, I returned to college to complete my bachelor's degree. After returning to ORU, I decided in my second semester that I was going to major in nursing and turn all the missions classes into a minor. It was time to focus on my medical education and start working at one of the hospitals in Tulsa to gain experience.

With a heavy heart, I submitted my resignation to the general manager and worked out an exit strategy regarding the timeline. He and the team were sad to see me leave but wished me success in pursuing my nursing education for the ultimate purpose of becoming a medical missionary. I had left the campus and secured a small apartment while I figured out my longer-term housing arrangements. During this transition time of working out my notice at the hotel and figuring out my long-term housing plan, I went to Michigan to attend my younger and only sister's wedding.

Life would throw me a curve ball as I met Gary Strobl, my future husband, during my visit to Michigan. After just 15 hours of having long conversations about our life experiences and dreams, he proposed. I knew in the depths of my heart Gary was the husband I had been praying to meet, and I said YES! I moved to Michigan, and we married about two months later.

Thankfully, I worked with ORU and found a way to keep all my college credits by changing my major to church administration to align with their long-distant learning program to finish my bachelor's degree remotely. Gary spoke often of his time in Georgia attending chiropractic school in Metro Atlanta, the good people he met, and fun times he had doing outdoor activities as a stress reliever through graduate school. We were able to move to Georgia to start a new life in 2003.

I worked for a staffing company out of necessity when we first moved to Georgia. One of these staffing agency assignments was at Georgia Marble as the administrative assistant to the vice president of sales. I enjoyed learning about business operations and sales as this was a whole new world for me. I thrived talking to our customers and working to improve communications between sales and operations. One day the vice president sent down several brochures, samples of the Marble that came out of the quarry, and a list of current customers. He was short of two business development managers, and said he was leaving to go on a two-week sales trip and needed a certain number of tombstone and mausoleum orders. He stressed the memorial division of the company we worked in desperately needed a revenue boost to avoid the parent company selling our division. He told me to figure out why Georgia Marble was superior to Italian marble, and to start calling customers and securing orders. He challenged me to see the WHY by taking a damp cloth and wiping off the tombstone of Colonel Stephen Clayton Tate (founder of Georgia Marble) who died in 1901. He guaranteed the tombstone would be in the same brilliant white, dense condition as the marble that had come out of the mine that day. I went to the cemetery and wiped off the tombstone. My boss was right!! That 102-year-old tombstone, once clean, looked just as brilliant as the marble I had seen earlier that day leaving the quarry. I immediately learned about each of our tombstone and mausoleum options, started making phone calls, and very quickly had the number of orders he requested. In that moment a light bulb turned on in my mind, that I had another talent—sales.

THIRD LEADERSHIP LESSON: Explaining the WHY and creating unique opportunities for those you lead to experience the WHY ignites an excitement inside those you lead to accomplish amazing things.

Despite our division's dramatic rise in revenue, we could not compete with the other division of the marble company that crushed marble into fine particles (calcium carbonate). Life changed again, and we were given notice our division would be closed. I found a job as an inside sales representative at the corporate office of a security guard company. I thought if could sell tombstones and mausoleums, I could learn another new industry. I worked hard to be the best in that role, gleaning every lesson I could from the director of the department, and others at the corporate office. There were times I thought the department could really soar if things were organized differently and certain policies were more employee focused.

One such policy impacted me heavily when Gary's father died. Since his father was not an immediate relative, the bereavement policy did not apply to me. I couldn't accompany him to the burial service for his father out of state. This broke my heart, and I can remember sitting at my desk the day Gary was burying his father, tears running down my face, praying for his comfort and promising God if I was given the opportunity to lead, I would provide more understanding and compassion to my team.

As if in answer to my prayers, an opportunity to say yes to leadership came knocking on my door again when our supervisor moved his family back to the northeast and his position became available. All my colleagues in the department applied for it except me. The director of the department called me into his office and asked why I had not applied. "Well, sir, I thought I was too young and the other team members would resent me becoming their manager as the relative new hire," I replied.

To my surprise, he encouraged me to apply because he said I had huge potential as a leader and my work ethic would be a tremendous asset in the role. "Your creativity, vision, intelligence, problem solving, collaboration skills, and insights from the other industries' best practices (marble mining, hospitality, food service, missions work overseas, non-profit leadership skills) would take the department to the next level of productivity." With that spark of encouragement, I applied.

After an extensive interview and testing process, I was promoted. I kept my promise to God and looked through the eyes of my employees when creating policies. I worked from an employee, faith-first perspective when balancing their roles within the directives of executive leadership. This leadership role stretched me tremendously. Not only was I growing to become a better leader, but that role grew into a manager role. This would be the beginning of a several decades-long security sales leadership career.

FOURTH LEADERSHIP LESSON: Leadership is a precious gift to be used wisely. It is not for the weak, but rather those individuals who choose to take the heat so a path can be made to help others shine.

It was during my security career journey that an opportunity to serve our community presented itself and Gary and I decided to join our local volunteer fire department. We both jumped on every opportunity to increase our knowledge. We attended EMT and firefighter schools during our nights and weekends to better position us in serving our community. Naturally, I started sharing my knowledge with my fellow firefighters in the department and to my surprise was appointed as the lieutenant of training.

This was a perfect position for me as I loved the role of creating training programs and engaging practical scenarios to apply our knowledge. Then our volunteer fire chief resigned, and my fellow firefighters debated whom they would consider as his replacement. We as a volunteer fire department had decreased our community outreach efforts and struggled to collaboratively work with the county fire department. Knowing I could bring my leadership knowledge to this role to help address these concerns, I stepped up and said I would be interested in serving as the volunteer fire chief.

Now, this was while I still worked my full-time security sales management role. I had no idea how I would balance both roles simultaneously, but the needs I saw within the department along with our community pushed me to serve. The lessons learned in previous leadership positions throughout my life gave me confidence to take the leap and use those lessons to make a difference in my community.

When the time came to vote for who would become our fire chief, all my male firefighters voted for me. I became the first female fire chief in my volunteer fire departments and county's history. It was a tremendous honor to serve my fellow firefighters and community in this role and there aren't words to express the gratitude that I have for the opportunity to lead and to learn.

FIFTH LEADERSHIP LESSON: Accomplishing amazing things cannot be achieved until we go beyond our comfort zone. We can impact lives positively when we leap out of that comfort zone and focus on meeting needs, placing service before ourselves, and lifting others up.

Pastors

Pastors are the ones who care
When it is hard for them to share.
They give of their time
And frequently give their last dime.
They sacrifice their life
So in their church there is no strife.
They stay in tune with God
So they can lift others when they feel lower than sod.
They show unending amounts of love
That doesn't push, demand or shove.
They're someone whom you can count on to care
When you desperately need someone
to help you escape your snare!

Inspiration

Church leaders of every kind do so much for their congregations, and sometimes it can be hard to know how to express the gratitude for the work they do. This poem was born to help people express their thoughts about the positive way pastors impact people's lives. If you have ever been at a loss for the words to express thanks, I hope you can use this poem to share your gratitude with the outstanding pastors and ministry leaders in your life.

Soldier

Soldiers loyally serve
And often endure more pain than they deserve,
They learn how to fight
And leverage their weapons of might,
They travel to foreign lands
And for ideas of freedom and human rights stand,
In the heart of War's strife
They sadly see some of their comrades lose their life,
They at times are torn with the things they see
And from the clutches of PTSD, they struggle to be free,
They operate at a different pace
And run their own kind of race,
They often think in a different way
And may struggle to find the right words to say,
They deserve our support and gratitude
So they can reach their highest altitude!

Inspiration

Throughout my career in security and fire service, I have met many soldiers. Each of their stories is unique and always gives me so much perspective about true selfless service. As many of us struggle with how to thank those who put their lives on the line every single day, I hope this poem gives you some words to express that gratitude. The sacrifices our soldiers make are deserving of our thanks and I pray that this poem will not only give you words to say thanks, but that it would encourage the soldiers no matter where they are in their military journey.

Public Safety Servants

Our world is kept safe and alive
Because they choose if needed to lay down their lives,
They work long hours
And often feel drained of their power,
The law enforcement officer battles crime
And often is paid very few dimes,
Firefighters mitigate fires and battle to rescue
those in vehicles or buildings trapped
Because of their training, they in
life-threatening situations can adapt,
EMS staff leverage their skills and equipment to keep patients alive
They face situations that can quickly take their lives,
Corrections officers do their best to help
others see a life can be transformed
They serve in a system doing its best to provide reform,
Wildland firefighters fight raging forest fires
They can as they fight these raging infernos heavily perspire,
These public servants must be observant
And in their commitment to service be fervent,
They frequently do their work in unsafe zones
And it easy for them to feel they are alone,
Let us spend more time to say THANK YOU
To these servants for all they do!

Inspiration

Since 2007, I have had the privilege of serving alongside amazing public safety leaders. This poem was written to honor those who choose to serve their communities in the many, many roles of public safety servants.

People

Texan

I am a Texan and am proud
Sometimes I am loud
I have a huge heart
That enjoys giving others a new start
I love my state
And my mate,
I am filled with hope
And gladly share it with others who are at the end of their rope,
I will always answer the call
To be a good friend to all.

Memories

Sometimes the words to my poems come when a friend needs them most. I wrote this poem after seeing on LinkedIn that my fellow security colleague, Charles "Chuck" Andrews MSME, CPP was going to be undergoing back surgery. Chuck has spent over forty years investing in others throughout his law enforcement and security careers. He even started a professional security network organization, "Friends of Chuck" (FOC), which exists for the purposes of networking, locating employment, exchanging business opportunities, discovering new emerging security technologies, and sharing the information that FOC members, your companies, and your organization need to know.

I thought about how he has been there for so many over the last several decades and how I could, with a poem, help bring a smile to his face during his recovery process. I hope these words help inspire you to help others, share hope, and be a friend just like Chuck Andrews and my many other Texas friends that have been a blessing to others.

Studying Student

As you are studying and feel like your brain is cooking, Here's some good home cooking!

Memories

This poem was written during the year I had to take off from ORU to raise more finances to complete my degree. Despite that time off, I was still very close to my friends on campus and communicated with them often.

During one of their final's weeks, many of them told me they were spending so much time studying, they felt their brains were being cooked. I may not have been on campus to lift them up, but I could still help. Those words inspired me to bake some cookies to share with my friends to help energize them as they prepared for finals.

The words of this poem were written on a scrap piece of paper while their cookies were baking in the oven. They were very surprised when I showed up with warm cookies fresh out of the oven on campus during finals week. This act of kindness quickly became a tradition in encouraging my friends. LIFE LESSON: Find what you DO HAVE and use that to bless others. More will come your way when you are willing to share your resources to bring hope to someone else.

Seniors

As the seniors graduate
They do anticipate
A life filled with hope
Held out on a rope.
When they arrive at graduation
Their hope will only be an infatuation
Unless they have Christ in their heart
From the start!

Inspiration

For many years, I have been blessed to mentor youth. I wrote this poem after spending many years mentoring young students and watching them progress through school until graduation day arrived. I can remember being in stores reading through countless cards and thinking they did not capture the words I wanted to share with the youth I knew who were graduating. I thought about when I was a senior graduating high school and how heavily I leaned on God for my hope in successfully navigating my adult life. My hope is that you can share these words with a graduating senior and encourage them in the next chapter of their life.

Special Days

Birthday

Happy birthday to a special someone on their day.
As you've walked through the years
And shed a few tears,
You've had a constant friend
Ready to take your broken heart and with love mend,
HE'S been there through the thick and thin
So you could win!

Memories

Many years ago, as I was signing a birthday card for a friend, I thought about what a blessing they were in my life and then the words of the poem freely flowed.

This poem also stands to remind us of what the precious gift our lives represent.

Growing up, my parents told me how I almost did not make it to my first birthday. They explained that as my first birthday approached, I became deathly ill with scarlet fever.

The fact you are reading this story today tells you that I recovered. Let us never forget how precious life is and celebrate our lives and the lives of those around us.

Valentine

God's Valentine was freely given
So men could be completely forgiven.
HE showed mankind a love
That didn't push and shove.
HE gave us a lasting hope based on
Faith and trust in HIS Son.
This Valentine was given an odd form
That simply was human adorned.
This unique and loving Valentine
Would empower us to have a transformed mind.
HE is alive forevermore
And has conquered death's shore.
HE loves us all
And will remove our heart walls.
Christ is our ultimate Valentine
Whose love is right on time.

Memories

Valentine's Day is often one that either brings great joy or deep sadness. Those who have a significant other in their life or loving family close by either have or appear to have great joy. But those without a significant other or without family close by can easily feel lonely and full of sadness.

The photo included with this poem is a smiling face cookie my husband bought for me from a store in Germany. We had just visited Neuschwanstein Castle. After our tour of this amazing castle, I fell while exiting the castle. I learned, upon returning home to the United States, that I had sustained two avulsion fractures as a result of the fall.

Just like my foot was broken and throbbed in pain, our hearts can experience the same. May this poem serve as a reminder that just like that cookie reflected my husband's love and concern for me, God has made a way to mend our broken hearts and replace the pain with HIS amazing love.

Thanksgiving

Thanksgiving is a time
When we remember all the year's dimes.
We look back and see God's hand
That helped us throughout the year to stand.
HE gave us energy
When we were filled with lethargy.
HE put food on our table
When we weren't able,
HE gave us hope
When we thought we could no longer cope,
HE watched over us
When we were in a great fuss.
HE once again kept us alive
So we could have another year to strive
To thank HIM for all HE does for us each day
Even if our day tends to sway.

Inspiration

This poem was written as a prayer of gratitude for all the miracles God has provided me.

May this poem serve as a challenge that we need to recognize and reflect on the miracles around us every day, not just during the holidays. What is your prayer or poem of Thanksgiving?

Christmas

One day long ago a Heavenly Babe was born.
As HE grew, HE was scorned.
HIS birth did bless the whole earth.
HE was and is the Savior who is of great worth.
It is a day that love should be freely given
To reflect God's ability to help us be forgiven,
Show others you care
And open your heart to share.

Inspiration

This poem was written as a reminder of Christ's impact on the earth. HE showed HIS followers compassion, mercy, love, forgiveness, and encouragement. The photo was taken during the first trip my husband and I took to Kolkata, India, to visit the children of the Hope Home in 2006.

What made the trip so much more special was that the children of the Sunday school class I taught back home had made Christmas cards for the children at Hope Home. They wrote messages of love and encouragement and shared their own families.

Many of the children at Hope Home decided to make cards for the American children back in Georgia. They wanted to share some love with the kids who took the time to send some love to them. This was a beautiful example of how we can open our hearts to share love during the holiday season and beyond. How can we share these precious gifts with others during the holiday season?

Places

Georgia

My home state
The pretty peach state
A place with mountains and steams
Where it is easy to dream
A state kissed with salty air
Along its wild beaches where you can explore if you dare
Where movies are made
And famous Hollywood individuals are paid
Where native pecans grow in the sunny heat
And the Stuckey's team transforms them into tasty treats,
Where people are kind
And are quick to help others who are in a bind,
A place where many meals are accompanied by tea that is sweet
And tables filled with culinary treasures to eat,
A place filled with diverse wildlife
And in the cities exciting nightlife,
A great state to call home
Where neighbors can be known,
One that is often on many minds
And friends are easy to find.

Memories

What does your moving history look like?

I have lived in three states so far in my life: Michigan, Oklahoma, and Georgia. I was born and raised in Michigan. Growing up I did not know a great deal about Georgia. That changed when I met Gary who had lived in Georgia and attended Life University in Atlanta. He completed graduate school and became a Doctor of Chiropractic.

We met and married in 2000. Our first Christmas together, we left the winter cold of Michigan to visit sunny Georgia. We visited the Life University campus to see the Christmas lights, Lake Lanier and Amicalola Falls State Park. I fell in love with the scenery, weather, food, and hospitality of Georgia immediately. I remember packing the trunk of the rental car to return home and saying to Gary I could not wait for us to find a way to leave our life in Michigan and start a new one in Georgia.

It took us three years after he took that photo to move to Georgia and start our new life. We came to the state with very little and yet throughout our time here this state has given us so much. Gary ended up with an interesting part-time career as an extra on hundreds of productions. He has helped people back onto the road of healing in their physical bodies as a Doctor of Chiropractic. Georgia was where my professional sales career soared; my security industry knowledge blossomed with obtaining ASIS International's Certified Protection Professional (CPP) Certification; the opportunity for Gary and me to serve our community as Volunteer State Registered Firefighters, licensed EMTs, and Explorer Advisors. We have had the pleasure of living in a beautiful community, and most importantly, we have made wonderful friends who have enriched our lives beyond measure.

This poem captures the things about my home state I love. It also recognizes the ability for entrepreneurial dreams to thrive in the state where Stuckey's was born.

This company was founded in 1937 by a man, who during the Great Depression, had a vision that was far bigger than the roadside pecan stand that started his business. Now his granddaughter, Stephanie Stuckey, is reviving this company along with a wonderful team of fellow Georgians. They are working hard to give the world tasty pecan snacks to take along on our own road trips. What next step do you want to take in life? What is holding you back?

USA

The nation where I was born
And too often feels torn,
A nation filled with people with different insights
That when united can make things right,
A place founded by those seeking a new life
And to be free from many kinds of strife,
A land overflowing with beautiful landscapes and wildlife
Whose splendor can bring some calm to life,
From sandy beaches
To majestic mountain peaks and their towering reach,
From miles of trees
To desert as far as the eye can see,
From large cities filled with hustle
To the rural areas free from all the bustle,
A place where with a grateful heart
It is possible to make a new start.

Inspiration

Travel has been part of my life and because of that I have traveled to many nations around the globe. Amidst all the beauty that other places have to offer, my heart continues to overflow with gratitude for the many blessings the United States of America has provided me and my family. This poem was composed to provide a more hopeful perspective of the nation I call home. How can you incorporate gratitude into your mindset regarding the place that you call home?

Canada

A land filled with golden streams
A nature lover's most beautiful dream,
A place to get away
And others have found a way to stay,
The land of mighty fish
That draws anglers filled with dreams of catching them
and eating them as a tasty dish,
A land filled with native people that against
the harsh elements have survived
They passed on their resiliency to their
descendants so they will thrive,
A place rich with adventurous history
And often shrouded in mystery,
A place overflowing with natural splendor
Whose majestic mountain peaks radiate grandeur,
A place alive with the sound of calling loons
Where many enjoy their unique tunes,
Where moose boldly walk the land
And tower above most when they stand,
A place that implores us to explore
And expand our horizons more,
Come see this special place
That has brought a smile to my face!

Inspiration

Canada is such a beautiful place, and this poem was written as I reflected on all the fishing trips my husband and I have made to this beautiful country since our first wedding anniversary. I never dreamed this was a place I would ever travel to and thanks to Gary, I have seen it often. Where have you traveled to that you never dreamed of going? Are there places that you dream of visiting?

India

Land of vibrant mystery
And a colorful, living history.
Slow moving cows
And sacred vows,
Fabrics rich with brilliancy
A people filled with resiliency.
The cities fill with hustle and bustle
While the vast countryside faintly hears a rustle.
Bengal tigers prowl and growl
While mischievous monkeys howl.
The Himalayas rise to their majestic peaks
While thrill seeking hikers scale for weeks.
The plains of hydria burn with heat
While hungry villagers search for meat.
The sacred Ghanges starts in high elevation
Bringing life and refreshing to the nation.
The Taj Mahal radiates with royalty
Speaking of a Prince's passionate loyalty.
The fields grow with delicious rice
Selling in the U.S. for a high price.
The people of India make her great
Opening wide their friendship gate.
A place some wish to flee
And others long to see.
Come and encounter her living history
While seeking to understand her mystery.

Memories

My first connection to India was an X-ray technician I met when I was volunteering as a candy striper in the largest emergency room in Tulsa, Oklahoma. We talked often of the struggles within his home country of India. My heart went out to the people he described, and it left me wondering how I could help.

Then I learned about a group of doctors and nurses who were going to Kolkata, India, for seven days (two days traveling and five days in country) to bring much-needed medical relief services to the people of Kolkata, India. This was exactly the opportunity I was praying for. I was so inspired by the work Mother Teresa's sisters were doing in the city and I wanted to be part of the team that went to Kolkata to help.

That was during the year I had to leave ORU to replenish my funds to return to school. I was working full time at the hotel as a front desk trainer and was able to persuade the general manager to give me the seven days off from work without pay. I promised to return as soon possible, because it was our busy season. I worked hard to raise all my funds for the trip and was ready to travel to Kolkata with the doctors and nurses.

With less than a month before I was scheduled to leave for India, the mission agency asked me to meet with them. They informed me that the doctors and nurses would not be able to make the trip, so they had cancelled it. Since I had already raised the money, they wanted instead to send me to Colombia for one month with an evangelistic team.

To say I was disappointed was an understatement. What was I going to tell everyone who had donated for a trip to India? I shared how I told everyone who had donated money for my trip how the funds were going to help people struggling with emergency medical issues in Kolkata. I was not comfortable telling those who trusted me with their money that it would now be diverted to Colombia.

What's more, I further explained about my financial situation with my employer. I had received approval for one week off and if I went to Colombia, I would not be paid for the entire month that I was away. I was without family or any other type of financial support. My employment at the hotel was my only source of income and I simply could not be gone for a month.

The mission agency searched through opportunities they had and found exactly what I needed. There was the option of still flying to Kolkata, India, but instead of being with a team, I would be headed there ALONE. They said that I could go during the dates I had already cleared with my employer.

The excitement of being able to make it to Kolkata was starting to build again. They explained that I would meet with a group of young adults who were already serving in the city. The group's mission was quickly ending, and they would be leaving the city two days after my arrival.

The agency representative let me know that I would go with them to schools to share about what God had done in my life. Then after they left the city, I would work with a local church group and serve at Mother Teresa's Kalighat Home for the Dying Destitutes. They would help me navigate through the city and return me to the airport at the end of the week. Without any thought, I said YES!

The only countries I had traveled to at that point were Jamaica, Haiti, and Venezuela. Boarding the 747 plane in Tulsa I remember praying, God, be with me on this entire trip and help me bring your hope to everyone I meet. The trip tested my physical resolve as the daily temperatures were over 115 degrees Fahrenheit. Not only that, but I became ill the first few days after reacting to the anti-malaria medication and a vaccine I had taken prior to entering the country.

Thankfully, I recovered from the reactions quickly and was able to join the team for the last day of their travels. The most humbling experience was when I met up with the local church to work in Mother Teresa's Kalighat Home for the Dying Destitutes. It made me appreciate the gift of life, and how important it is to live your life without regrets. India was amazing and I fell in love with the people, culture, and food. When I returned home to Tulsa, I made sure to stay in touch with the local church group that I had served with. I dreamed of returning to share more hope and love.

The very next year I married Gary and he heard all about my travels to Kolkata and my desire to return. Thankfully, I remained in contact with the leader of the church group I had worked with during that first trip. They had since started a children's home, and in 2006 Gary and I went together to serve.

That trip started a yearly tradition over the next several years of my using two to three weeks of my vacation time. It was such a blessing to be able to take a break from my full-time career managing the Inside Sales Team at U. S. Security Associates to visit the children's home (Hope Home) in Kolkata, India with Gary. I wrote this poem many years after no longer making these trips due to the expense and the political changes at the time within Kolkata. The takeaway from my story for you is there are needs around us every day, regardless of what city, state, or country we are in at that moment. Each of us has resources and a smile we can share to brighten someone's world. Join me in opening our eyes to the needs around us and finding ways to help meet those needs.

Grace

Amazing Grace

Amazing grace, amazing grace
It enables me to seek God's face.
How sweet to my weary soul
When the stresses of life take their toll.
It picks me up
When I want to give up.
God's grace is so amazing
Because it is beyond my understanding.
It enables me to stand before a Holy God
When I feel lower than sod.
It points me to the amazing depths of God's love
And reminds me of the gift God gave from above.
I cannot fathom God's amazing grace
I can boldly approach His throne of grace!

Inspiration

Some moments stay with us more than others. I wrote this poem remembering the time I sang this hymn at the graveside of an amazing woman. She was like a grandmother to me when I was young, and she spoke so much life into me. She and her husband had been missionaries to Africa and during one such trip there, her husband passed away.

When we would visit, she would tell me stories over tea. Stories about her faith in Christ pulling her through times of utter despair and deadly sickness. Her faith through so many adversities made a huge impact on me and my faith. She always encouraged me to dream big, to never lose my faith in Christ, to always believe God had an amazing plan for my life, and to never fear speaking before others. She told me often, "The world needs more of God's grace and love." She told me to boldly embrace any opportunities HE gave me to share HIS message of hope. I sang this song to her with tears in my eyes and love in my heart for her. She was such an amazing woman who truly touched my life.

Grace

Unconditional, eternal grace
Only comes from one place.
It comes from God's son
Who is risen and has won.
HE does not fill us halfway and stop
But HE fills us with his grace all the way to the top.
God's grace is always there
When we need someone to care.
So when we need God's grace
We must look to HIS face!

Inspiration

We often are very hard on ourselves when things don't go the way we thought or planned. Not only that, but we are quick to see others' faults. I wrote this poem out of overwhelming gratitude to God for helping me to forgive myself when I missed the mark. For always giving me unmerited assistance when I did not deserve it and giving me compassion to show others the grace I have received. What is one mistake you can forgive yourself for today? To whom can you extend grace today?

Joy

Smile

Smile, smile, smile
Cause God's love will go that extra mile.
Praise God
Because HE lifts us up when we feel like sod.
Pray every day
So God will point us to his way!

Memories

From an early age, I expressed the joy I was feeling in my heart with a big smile. As I got older, I soon learned that people around me who were struggling with sadness, depression, and anger found my enthusiasm problematic. Growing up, my abundant enthusiasm often was not the norm nor was it welcome. I was encouraged to fit in the more traditional box of behavior like those around me.

My peers and the adults in my life would ask me to "tone it down." I was criticized for my voice being loud, my face being too expressive, and my smile too big. During those formative years of happiness oppression impacted me as I moved into my teenage years. I smiled less, was frequently silent, spoke less, felt self-conscious, and became very depressed. There were times that hiding who I really was for the sake of others made me suicidal. Internally I was in anguish, struggling to understand why I did not fit in.

My enthusiasm began to return when I started going on mission trips and serving my local community. During my first mission trip to Jamaica, the two deaf teenagers on my team (for whom I frequently served as interpreter because I was fluent in sign language) told me how my smile encouraged them during times they were nervous being so far away from home. During a mission trip to Valencia, Venezuela, I was responsible for two teenagers and another young adult who struggled with a developmental disorder. They had never been outside of the United States. They shared how my enthusiasm lessened their homesickness and helped them focus on helping the people of Venezuela.

I couldn't communicate in Bengali or Hindi to the very ill people at the Mother Teresa's Kalighat Home for the Dying Destitutes in Kolkata, India; but my smile became my most precious communication tool to convey love as their lives hung in the balance. I may not have had words, but that smile was full of love and hope.

Even during my time as a candy striper at the largest emergency room in Tulsa, people would often thank me for my smile and enthusiasm as it helped and encouraged them during their emergency moments. As the years flew by, and I continued to step out into new professional and community volunteer roles, I realized that the very thing (my smile) I thought was a curse was a gift I had been given to connect people with hope. What is your unique trait? How can you use it to help others?

Stress

In our life stress can make a big mess
But our Heavenly Father is always ready to bless.
Stress can tie our stomach in knots
But HE can love us a lot.
Stress to our heart can be extremely bad
But He can make our hearts exceedingly glad!

Inspiration

This poem was written during some of the most stressful moments of my life as a reminder that by laying my burdens down in prayer, peace could be found. What stress are you facing today?

Faith

The Eyes of Jesus

HE always sees and never questions.
HE will never tease and does not need an introduction.
These actions and eyes belong to a man who has run HIS life on
Earth without strife,
So that by HIS name we might win!

Memories

This is the first poem I ever wrote at the age of 17. It was while I was in Jamaica with 29 other teenagers and four adults building a water tank for a school for deaf children. I remember when a representative from a mission agency came to our church and talked about the various trips they had available for youth to participate in around the world over the summer. I loved the idea of going overseas and being part of a team that would build something to meet critical needs long-term to help children have a new life of education.

The brochure advised we would spend three weeks at a boot camp just outside of Miami learning the skills needed to construct the water tank at the children's deaf school in Jamaica. Then we would spend about two months in Jamaica living at the deaf school while constructing the water tank and sharing God's love with the deaf school children. After our two months and the completion of the water tank, we would return to the mission agency's headquarters for a week to debrief before returning home.

This would be my first trip outside of the United States. It would prove to be a game changer in my life in many ways. During boot camp we stayed in tents, and I learned about masonry. Sweating in the humid Florida summer heat, battling insects, and learning more about my fellow teammates provided a challenging experience. It didn't matter, though, because we all thought this rough living was only temporary. We would have great living conditions in Jamaica.

We flew into Montego Bay, Jamaica, and traveled by bus for several hours to the deaf school site. Once we arrived on that rainy evening, we realized the deaf school was empty. We teenagers were expecting something much different from what stood before us. Outside of the dark school was a missionary couple and their little girl.

Why were there no deaf children at the school? Well, the residential school was not open yet because there was no clean water source. The missionaries had converted a small portion of the empty building into their home. The rest of the building was a basic two story, cement structure without doors or windows. There was a little pavilion with tables and chairs where we could eat our meals or get out of the sun.

The missionaries let us know that there was no plumbing and no bathroom facilities at the school. The only source of water was the rainwater that was captured in large, metal five-gallon drums. A layer of worms had to be skimmed off the top of these rain barrels to access the water, and then the water was boiled to be safe to consume. Our thoughts on toughing out the heat and bugs in Florida changed quickly as we slept on the cement floor of the school those first few days. Thankfully, the local Jamaican men came and helped us figure out where we could set up our tents. They also worked to help clear the jungle vegetation, so we had a flat area for the tents. Once that was cleared, we set up the boundaries for the area of the jungle which would serve as our "bathroom" during the next few months. Our bathing area was a several-mile walk to the nearby river where we would bathe and do our laundry once a week.

With our basics laid out, we soon realized the materials to build the water tank on top of the mountain (above the deaf school) had not arrived. The small retainment water tank behind the deaf school that would hold water coming from the large water tank we would be building was also not completed. But we would not be swayed by struggles. Very quickly we jumped into being a construction crew, finishing the small water tank beside the deaf school, with limited water, food and very basic housing accommodations.

In addition, when the dump trucks full of our materials could not make it up the mountain, we became a road crew, leveling the road with our shovels so the trucks could get closer to the site. That made the task of unloading all the cement blocks and other necessary materials just a bit easier. Next up was digging the latrine at the top of the mountain we would use while we worked on the water tank.

Once we finished all this work, we could finally start on the water tank project. Unfortunately, we were about a month behind schedule. We were able to construct most of the water tank, minus the roof and floor. We would spend five to six days a week from sunrise to sunset (minus a three-hour lunch break) completing this labor-intensive work in the hot Jamaican sun, then at night collapse in our tents.

This type of work quickly weakened my body, and I became deathly ill. It was during this time when I wondered how I was going to make it that the words of this poem flooded my mind. These words filled me with hope and God healed my body to finish our mission in constructing the water tank. The school (www.jcsdeaf.org) is still open today, transforming the lives of deaf and disabled children. I hope this poem encourages you to see you are not alone, and with God's help you can win, in even the most difficult of situations.

Peace

Where can we find everlasting,
Comforting peace?
It can be found in Christ,
The Prince of Peace!

Inspiration

This poem was written for me as a reminder that life, as a follower of Christ, is best lived when we remember we are not alone. That during the hard days of struggle and anxiety, HE is there to help us navigate our journey with HIS love, grace, and peace. What burden can you give to God in prayer today?

Friends

There is a friend I know
Who did sink very low.
HE took the world's sins
So that HIS future children might win.
You ask who could this be?
Well, HE is no stranger to me.
This eternal friend has lived since the beginning of time.
HE made salvation mine
This eternal friend's name is Jesus, Prince of Peace.

Inspiration

Friendship is a word that is used often and at times is misunderstood. Each of us has had a friendship that did not grow into the relationship we envisioned. It is easy to carry hurt in our hearts from these painful moments. This poem was written during Easter as I reflected on Christ's resurrection and how that truth has impacted my life. It reminded me that not only did it mean I could be forgiven of my sins, but that Christ is the eternal friend I can depend on consistently. Let this poem encourage you to lay the hurt at Christ's feet so HE can heal your heart and be the friend you have always wanted and needed. One that sticks closer to you than a brother or sister.

The One

Seek the ONE who can take your cares that worry you a ton,
Call out to HIM who can help you in life's troubling waters swim.
Hold tightly the hand
Of the ONE who can give you power to stand.
Look to the shining son
Who against evil has won.
Who is this mighty ONE
Who shines brighter than the sun?
Christ is HIS name
And HIS healing, delivering power
Will always be the same.

Inspiration

I wrote this poem years ago in church after I heard someone requesting prayer for a family member who was struggling. I remember hearing the concern in her voice for her family member. I prayed for her family member silently, but in my heart, I wanted to offer more words of comfort.

As I prayed, these words flooded my mind. I wrote the words on a notecard in my Bible and gave this poem to her after church. She had tears in her eyes and a smile on her face after reading the poem. My heart overflowed with gratitude to God for giving me these words to help encourage her and her family members in their journey. It is amazing what a few encouraging words can do to bolster our faith and give us just a bit more hope than we had before.

Race

In this life we run a race
The Christian runs it with God's grace,
We place our faith in HIS power
Trusting HIM to give us strength for each hour,
Because they know peace and hope will come at God's pace.
The race is many times constant push and shove
But we know that we always have access to God's love!

Inspiration

This poem was written as a reminder that while we run the good race of life, God stands ready to provide us HIS grace, hope, and peace to help us along the journey. HE is our coach cheering us on along the way, and he is ready to jump in with replenishment and encouragement, so we do not quit. Where are you in life's race? I'm praying for you today; be strengthened and DON'T GIVE UP!

Lord

To you
I am not new,
Unto you I tightly cling
For you take away my pain's sting.
You hold me
And daily love me,
Soothing my broken heart
And giving it a brand new start.
Thank you Lord for being there
To wipe away each and every tear!

Inspiration

When I was living in Tulsa, Oklahoma, and following my dream to attend Oral Roberts University, I was officially on my own. I can remember struggling with my major, and the sadness of my family not supporting my move to attend the university. The feeling of loneliness felt overwhelming at times. Then, I had a meeting with one of my professors who had lived overseas as a missionary with his family. Out of the blue, he asked if I had any prayer requests. After I shared my struggles, I felt as though a weight was lifted, as if I just needed to speak my burdens out loud.

He smiled. "God guided you to this school and HE will be faithful in continuing to guide you in your education as long as you keep asking HIM for help." He reminded me that God loved me and would be my closest friend during the darkest of times. I was not alone, and you are not alone either. I am praying for you in this moment that you would know that God loves you and that HE is here for you too.

Day

Today is a brand-new day
Full of things and circumstances ready to sway.
A day in which I may fear,
Because I might have a tear.
One that I don't want to really face
Because of the quick, changing pace.
A day for which I have no energy
And want to dwell in lethargy,
I know in the depths of my soul
It will take its toll.
Also, I know that my God can do anything
And nothing is too difficult for HIM, nothing.
HE is the same yesterday, today, now and forever
And HE has given me the lever
To face this day with the strength and words to pray:
Lord, carry me this busy day.
Then, in turn HE will hear my prayer
And take my burdens
Not letting them in my heart tear.
HE will hold me
Until I clearly see
HIS everlasting love
That doesn't shove
But surrounds me
Like the never-ending sea!

Memories

Life takes unexpected turns and sometimes those turns can change our lives. See, this poem was written during one of the many sad days I struggled through after my college roommate, Christian "Christie" Hoesli, was killed in a head-on collision during Christmas break. Sadness filled my days, and I struggled for many months after her death. It felt impossible to understand why at 18 her life ended so suddenly.

Crying out and praying to God, I asked for HIS comfort when all I could feel was pain. Why? Why did I have to lose my dearest friend at such a young age?

The words of the poem flooded my mind during this time and encouraged me to trust God to carry me through another day while HE helped my broken heart to heal. The photo I selected, taken in my community, reminded me of the light of hope God filled my heart with during those moments in prayer. May this poem fill your heart with hope when facing difficult days.

Faith

Faith is a powerful tool
That isn't found in school.
It's made up of things hoped for
That lie on a desolate shore.
It only is a strong tower
When we place it in God's power.
It's an anchor in our life
When we're surrounded by strife.
It draws us to God
When we feel as low as sod.
Faith opens our eyes
To a hope that will never die.
Faith is the substance of a radical life
Cleansing us from all our strife!

Inspiration

Sometimes we need reminders of the simple things. For me, this poem was written to remind me that through all the challenging times I have had in my life, my faith in God has been the constant factor in helping me succeed. My faith in HIM has helped me navigate the sea of life.

Answers

I know someone who has the answer
To all things and conditions such as cancer.
HIS answers many times aren't appealing
But they are flesh-revealing.
HIS answers change lives
While ours produce negative vibes.
HIS answers bring a satisfying soul peace
That will never cease.
HE stands ready with answers and the power
to give your life a new start.
Today let HIS love fill your heart!

Inspiration

This poem was written to fan the flames of my faith while I experienced difficult times or watched as others endured tremendous hardships. The poem helped me to shift my focus from the trials and struggles to God's love and power to turn the tide.

Live

Born to die
Die to live
To live for Christ, even when you feel at the end of your rope
Is to live full of hope.
To live serving the Master
Is to find peace in disaster.
To praise the risen Savior
Is to discern God's favor.
To pour your life into others
Is to see God love them like no other.
To take up your cross
Is to count the cost.
To surrender all
And completely answer God's call
Is finding life
And being delivered from all your strife.
Only in Christ do I find
Freedom from my fearful mind!

Inspiration

These words came to me as a reflection of my love for God. They hold the gratitude I have for all the times HE brought peace to my heart. They serve as a reminder that our lives are meant to be about so much more than wealth or fame. What are you living for each day?

Stand

Take a firm stand
When compromise is as numerous as sand.
Hold fast to the Master
And avoid impending disaster.
Live a life of integrity
And do not fear a life of obscurity.
Stand with a life of purpose
And have depth beyond the smiling surface.
Stand for your loving Savior
When all you see around you is compromising behavior,
Stand in purity
Resting in God's security,
Stand for Christ
And HE will take you to new heights.
Stand with the Bright Morning Star
And HE will take you far!

Memories

Just about an hour outside of my hometown in Michigan (where I grew up) was a community college. Many of us who have traveled the college road know that you can knock out your core classes at the less expensive community college before you transfer to your university of choice. That is exactly what I was doing.

Once I completed my core classes, I planned to transfer to Oral Roberts University to pursue a nursing degree with a strong emphasis on utilizing that education overseas to help needy individuals. I remember registering for the speech class and being excited to take it because I was already comfortable speaking in front of people since I had been doing so since I was a kid.

You may have already read in another poem that my father was a pastor when I was very young. Well, he started me off public speaking young. Every Sunday, when I was just five years old, he would let me give a mini-sermon from my picture bible. That was my first public speaking experience, and I loved it!

Even at such a young age, I found public speaking rewarding. It meant being able to share encouraging messages with people and seeing how it positively impacted their lives. As I got older, I continued saying yes to opportunities to speak encouraging messages at other churches during my childhood. I spoke as the chapter leader during InterVarsity Christian Fellowship meetings which met on the campus of the community college where I was taking the speech class.

We received an assignment to select two to four poems from the few poetry book choices the teacher had recommended. Many of the poems I read in these books seemed depressing. Something VERY not me.

I brought this very thing up to my professor, letting her know I did not feel comfortable presenting these poems for my speech. Since the speech needed to be based on our review of several poems, I asked if I could use two to four of my poems to present to the class.

Curious, the teacher asked me what kind of poems I wrote, and I shared that my poems were about how God had helped me through difficult times or how I felt about HIS work in the world around me. She asked me why I had that perspective, and I mentioned my belief that God had significantly intervened in my life up to that point. She allowed me to use my poems for my speech under the requirement I did not seek to convert anyone or emphasize any one religious per-spective. I focused my presentation on reading my poems, sharing my inspiration in writing them, and encouraging other classmates to see writing poetry as an opportunity to express their feelings when life can seem confusing.

As I prepared to present my speech in class, I remember being a little anxious about sharing my poetry. This would be the first time I was sharing it with strangers. In that moment, my nervousness was replaced with the words of this poem as it flooded my mind. I jotted this poem down quickly as I finalized my speech on the other poems I had selected for the presentation. The speech was a success, and I got an A! The lesson I leave you with is do not fear being bold! Be ready to create opportunities to share your talents outside the comfort zone.

Leap

I took the leap
And my safe zone and comfort I did not keep
I answered God's call
Trusting HE would not let me fall
I choose not to be overwhelmed by fear
Even when others jeered
I am now on the other side
Trusting God will turn my tide

Inspiration

There are defining moments for us all. This poem was written to encourage a security colleague of mine. She left her role in corporate America as the chief security officer for a global company to follow the many dreams Christ had put in her heart. She took the leap to make a difference in the world for HIM.

Each of us has unique talents that we can use to make a difference in our communities and in the lives of those around us. May this poem encourage you to leap into leveraging your talents in a whole new way to make a positive impact everywhere you go!

Love

Together

We are forever together no matter what the weather.
Our hearts are forever tied and will never die.
We have come as one under the compassionate Son.
We pledge to unite when we are tempted to fight.
Together we will be when the future we can't see.
Together is our battle cry when from
this world we must say goodbye.
Together serving our conquering king
who has made our hearts to sing.
Together we place our hope in the ONE who will help us cope.
Together we place our trust in God's kingdom which does not rust.
Together we start our life
Holding the hand of the ONE who wipes away our strife!

Memories

Generational bondage can be harrowing. Many of us see how our loved ones grew up and vow to be different. It wasn't different for me, as I grew up seeing many of the women in my family struggle in their relationships to feel truly loved and appreciated for who they were and their unique talents. I made a choice early on that was not going to be my story.

As a teenager, I prayed for my future husband, and I would see us working together to help others in need. I also asked God to fill my heart with an abundance of His love so that I would have an abundance to share with my future spouse.

As I moved into my twenties, I had not met anyone whose traits checked all the boxes of the man I wanted to marry. After seeing the unhappiness that followed so many women I knew, I decided that I would rather never marry if I couldn't marry the person who would love me completely, support my dreams, have a heart of compassion, and most importantly would serve those who were hurting with me.

I increased my involvement with volunteer organizations serving at-risk youth and others in Tulsa. This helped me to turn my focus away from feeling lonely while my peers were in relationships. It turned my focus outward toward others who had critical needs. I didn't know it then, but Gary, my future husband had also decided that he would rather remain single than marry a woman who was not right for him.

Gary was a Doctor of Chiropractic working in Port Huron, Michigan, as an Independent Contractor Doctor of Chiropractic at another chiropractor's office. He was also preparing to start working a few nights a week at a hotel. One of his patients was the new general manager of the hotel and she was having trouble finding a reliable employee to work the front desk during the 11 p.m. - 7 a.m. shifts.

Little did we know that we were about to meet one another. I was 25 years old, and he was 30 years old. Living in Tulsa, I was in the process of settling into a new apartment off campus and I was preparing to change my major to nursing in the fall so I could be better prepared for a medical missionary career. My younger and only sister was getting married in Michigan during this time. She wanted me to attend the wedding as her maid of honor.

The general manager of the hotel where I was still working offered me the opportunity to stay at a hotel that had just opened that was managed by the same company that owned our property. He asked me to find out how the property was doing and in exchange, he would give me an employee room rate of $25 per night. Well, that settled it, and I packed up and headed to Michigan to attend my sister's wedding.

The night I checked in, Gary was working behind the desk of the hotel that my general manager had reserved for me at the employee rate. It was only Gary's second day on the job, so he had not been trained on checking in a guest with an employee rate. Luckily for us both, the hotel utilized the same computer system, so I was able to show him how to enter the employee rate.

We talked for several hours that evening, realizing each of us had several of the traits we were seeking in a spouse. Right before I stepped on the elevator to go to my room for the night, he asked me to join him for lunch the next day by the river in town. I happily agreed. We had a picnic by the river the next day and talked for several more hours about our dreams.

It was such a rare meeting of souls that we quickly realized that God had brought us together. After just 15 hours of knowing each other, Gary proposed, and I said yes. We prayed together at the river, dedicating our lives together to God and asking him to work out the details so we could be married. God answered our prayers and we set our wedding date for September 2, 2000. We decided to have a small ceremony with immediate family and a few close friends at a park we had found during a drive along the coast overlooking Lake Huron.

We decided on that specific park after seeing an amazing sight. During our visit, when we walked down to the beach that the park overlooked, we saw two white swans on the lake close to shore. We felt that this moment was something special because swans mate for life. Our wedding invitations had a swan on the front as a tribute to this moment. I knew our being brought together to be married was through divine intervention and that God had big plans for us together.

I wanted to capture this miracle in a poem to share with the small group of our immediate family who attended the wedding. Thus, this poem was created. May this story and poem inspire you to believe that God loves you and can do miracles in providing you opportunities for beautiful relationships.

God's Love

God's love is one size fits all.
HIS love will answer to any call.
Whether we call out to him day or night
HE takes away all of our frights.
HE never forces his love our way.
Instead, when we ask HE puts it in our hearts to stay.
So whether you feel very loved
Or totally and utterly unloved,
God's love will touch you
And HE will let you know that
HE loves you true and true!

Inspiration

Our world is often filled with hurt, hopelessness, and hurry. It is easy during these moments to feel unloved. This poem was written as a reminder that no matter the loneliness or sadness that may sweep over us, our Heavenly Father loves us. May you find hope in this truth today.

God

God is a loveable and huggable God.
HE is always touchable.
HE does not condemn us
But instead, HE loves us.
HE is readily there
When our cares become too much to bear.
So if you need God's love,
Look to the God who is as gentle as a dove!

Inspiration

You have read on this journey thus far many times when I faced extremely difficult situations. God listened to each prayer and answered them in HIS way. Sometimes I did not understand HIS ways or timing regarding the answers. The one thing that was constant was the truth that I could bring my burdens to HIM in prayer. What burden are you carrying that is keeping you from feeling God's love?

Fight

When you love someone, you and they tend to fight
Because it seems your right.
The heart is not healed by it.
Instead, fighting tears it.
The only way we can stop fighting
Is to look to God's love that is so inviting.
His love is never-ending.
It's always very mending!

Inspiration

Our world is often filled with messages that highlight our differences and view them as a source of strife. It is far too easy to focus on what makes us different instead of remembering all the things we love about those closest to our hearts. This poem serves as a reminder that only love heals hearts and makes relationships strong. God offers an abundance of love to heal our hearts that have been damaged and bruised from strife. What relationship in your life needs mending? What steps can you take to show more love and understanding in that relationship?

Who

Who is the love of my life
Taking away all my strife?
Who protects me at night
When the air is filled with frights?
Who loves me, no matter what
When my heart is severely cut?
Who calms my heart's fears
When I've been shedding tears?
Who overfills my heart with gladness,
Taking away all my sadness?
HE is my very best friend
That has a character that never bends.
HIS name is Jesus Christ
Who is the all-loving and all-knowing Christ!

Inspiration

This poem reflects the gratitude I have for Christ who, since I started serving HIM when I was young, has been a constant companion throughout my life. May this poem serve as a lighthouse of hope during your journey. I pray you discover that HE stands ready to be your companion and will lend you a helping hand to navigate life's challenges.

Love

Love is a force
That's stronger than a horse.
It compels the deepest devotion
When we are void of emotion.
It binds many hearts
To a Savior who abounds with love and
can give broken hearts a new start.
HE loved us so much that HE stretched out his arms and died
So we from death and despair no longer have to hide.

Inspiration

The words of Christ in John 15:13 inspired this poem: "Greater love hath no man than this, that a man lay down his life for his friends." Christ showed us the ultimate picture of love throughout his life on earth and by bearing our sins on the cross so we could be forgiven. He is ready to offer us forgiveness, hope, and healing. Who can you share this kind of life-changing love with today?

His Love

God's love binds
Together the brokenness of hearts
By letting them love again with a new start.
HIS love showers our souls with a precious peace
Which guards our hearts and minds and never ceases.
HIS love gives us the ability to care
When we do not want to even dare.
HIS love looks beyond all we have done
And points us to HIS loving Son.
HIS love is never conditional
But rather always unconditional.
HE loves us for who we are
And tenderly heals our emotional scars.
HIS love is free and unending
And is also heart-soul mending.
HIS love helps us to stop condemning ourselves
And enables us to forgive ourselves.
HIS love reaches the depths of our soul
Mending, restoring, and healing our weary soul.
HIS love goes beyond our minds
Bringing us through the toughest of binds.
God's love is something we all need
Because only HE can meet our wanting-to-be-loved needs.
If you desire this priceless and eternal love
Look to your caring and loving God above.
HE will come into your heart
And give you a brand-new start!

Inspiration

As humans, we make mistakes and poor choices all too often. These mistakes can result in consequences that leave us feeling ashamed and hopeless.

This poem serves as a light to remind us that change is possible. If we have breath, it is not too late to make things right. Christ can help us forgive ourselves, free us from condemnation, and empower us to start a new life. How can you help others avoid the mistakes you made in your life?

He's There

Christ is always there
When we need someone to desperately care.
HE always calms our many fears,
Even when we've been shedding tears.
HE opens our eyes to a way of life
That can be lived without any strife.
HE gives us a deep joy
That doesn't fade like a new toy.
HE gives us a lasting hope
That doesn't slip like a bar of soap.
HE gives us a lasting peace
That doesn't expire like a lease.
HE loves us with a love
That doesn't push and shove.
HE is like no other
Sticking closer than a brother.
HE is the Prince of Peace
Whose grace will never cease!

Inspiration

Sometimes we need a reminder that God will always be there. This poem was written as a reminder of how the words of Deuteronomy 31:8 have continued to ring true in my life: "And the Lord, he it is that doth go before thee; he will be with thee, he will not fail thee, neither forsake thee: fear not, neither be dismayed."

Christ has been the constant friend who was there for me throughout my life. Let these words bring hope to your heart, that no matter the loneliness you may feel, there is an eternal friend who can carry you through your darkest night.

God Loves You

Roses are red
Violets are blue
God sees you
As one of a kind
A person who he wants to find.
HE searches for you
When you are feeling blue,
So HE can tell you and show you
Just how much HE loves you.
HE is waiting lovingly and patiently
To receive you
And all you have to do
Is run to HIS open arms
And repent from all your harms!

Inspiration

This is a simple message that I hope will make you smile and warm your heart with hope. You are not alone and are valued. Who can you bring a smile to and help feel valued today?

Hope

Cries

Even though you may cry
And your throat may be dry,
Christt will always bear
Your each and every care,
As long as you say
Lord, take this day!

Inspiration

What are you struggling with today?

This poem was written during my late high school years when I struggled with frequent illnesses and rejection by those around me. They didn't understand the dreams I had within my heart.

During these struggles, I would find a quiet place to pray. Pouring out my heart to God would lift the burden from my heart and give me strength to navigate another day.

What has filled your eyes with tears? Where is your quiet place to give your burdens to God in prayer?

If you are struggling with pain and heartache, know I am praying for you.

Lonely Heart

Sometimes dear friends seem so far away,
And we want to be with them instead of wanting to stay.
During these times we hear the Lord gently say,
Aren't you going to pray?
So we bring our lonely heart to the place of prayer
And we see and feel the Lord most assuredly there.
Then as we talk to the Prince of Peace
HE floods our heart with His everlasting peace!

Inspiration

So many times in our lives we will endure struggle. This poem was penned during my year away from ORU. I was working multiple jobs to make ends meet and missing my friends on campus. I felt lonely without the support of my family and missed the few friends back in Michigan who had encouraged me to follow my dreams of attending ORU.

These words served as a tremendous encouragement as I navigated these difficult times. May these words bring you comfort in your times of loneliness. May they remind you that Christ can brighten your heart with the light of HIS love.

Way

Christ can make a way
When you're facing your darkest day.
A light can shine in your night
When your future is filled with fright.
HE can deliver you from your hell
Even though you fell.
A trumpet can sound with hope
When you are in the depths of despair and can no longer cope.
HE can free you from addiction
And through HIS mercy remove all condemnation.
HE can give us peace
So we can from our strife cease.
HE can show us the way
To abide in HIS hope every day!

Inspiration

The words of this poem serve as a reminder that hope lives. Often, we stay frozen in fear and believe there is no way out of our situations. Let these words point you to prayer and seeking Christ who can show you the way to hope and healing.

Forever

Forever, a word that we can't understand
Unless guided by God's loving hand.
Forever speaks of a time in which Jesus's glory will brightly shine.
Forever speaks of a bind that eludes our human mind.
Forever speaks of a commitment we try
to keep among our deep human ties.
Forever shows an act of love that could
only be given from God above.
Forever victory is what Jesus thought of when on the cross he
made Satan's hold on death and sin history.
Forever is the sign for hope for those who feel they can't cope.
Forever shows the soul-satisfying love that's available to all
because of a gift from above.
Forever reminds us of the gift of Jesus who brings peace, joy and
security to needy souls.
Forever speaks of Jesus's character that never changes.
Forever draws us to a God who will pick
anyone out of the lowest pit of sod.
Forever shows a love that does not draw racial lines
and is faithfully color-blind.
Make forever part of your soul daily by giving your heart to Jesus
Christ, forever personified!

MEMORIES OF
A VIBRANT LIFE

CHRISTIAN MARIE
HOESLI

April 3, 1981 — December 18, 1999

Memories

After a year off from ORU to save the money for tuition and the return to campus, my life was changed forever. I was placed in the freshman dorm and three weeks into the semester, Christi (Christian) became my roommate. Our dormitory wing's name was SOZO, a Greek word meaning salvation, deliverance, or to be saved. We never dreamed of the significance this word's meaning would have for us at the end of the semester.

Christi was navigating her first semester of college far from her family and friends in Michigan. As we became friends, she shared her dream of being a news reporter and a TV anchor. She loved the outdoors and sports. So it was no surprise when she quickly became involved with our wing's intramural football team.

She loved life and made her friends a priority. She prayed often and was known across campus for her long prayers and the peace that would come across her face during those prayers. She continuously sought out ways to creatively encourage others.

Her incredible compassion touched my life when, early in the semester after running 1,000 miles a minute to pack up my life from the previous year away from campus, leaving my apartment, and living in half of a tiny dormitory room, I found my body exhausted and ill with a severe cold. Christi prayed for me often. She surprised me with a card that said, "' The Lord bless thee, and keep thee.' Numbers

6:24. Hello! Jesus loves you, This I know, for the Bible tells me so. Get well soon. LOVE CHRISTIAN."

She radiated love wherever she went and made those around her feel special. She never said anything negative, even in times of frustration. Toward the end of the semester, she really started to miss her life back in Michigan and wanted to finish out her college education closer to home. She missed her family, her church, and her friends too much to remain at ORU.

She told us in the SOZO wing that she would not return to school after Christmas break. She had significantly impacted our lives and we were very sad to see her go. I knew I could return to Michigan where I grew up and visit her during break.

So, on the day she left school, she thanked me for everything, and we hugged. Truly, it did not seem like a forever goodbye. But it was. I received the call on December 18, 1999, from Christi's mom that she had been killed instantly in a car accident in Michigan. My heart sank and I physically sank to the floor of my dorm room.

I couldn't believe it. She was just here. I was numb hearing the words that Christi was gone from earth forever. Her mom let me know about the funeral arrangements and I was not able to coordinate leaving work to attend. The pain in my heart intensified when the reality hit me that I would not be attending her funeral service.

The employer helped me take a handful of days off to return to Michigan after Christmas and visit Christi's family. My sister was there to help me drive once I picked her up at my parents' home en route to the Hoesli family's home. That was a hard trip for me emotionally and I appreciated my sister being there as I was deep in the middle of grieving. After my visit, I returned to campus that next semester and worked with the SOZO wing to schedule a memorial service for Christi on the campus of ORU. I knew she had touched so many lives and I wanted everyone to have the chance to remember her impact on campus.

As I designed the memorial service, I still struggled to understand why my 18-year-old roommate was no longer on this earth. That is when the words of this poem flowed. I thought about how Christi lived her life and the many other youth who at her funeral gave their hearts to Christ seeking salvation.

The Greek meaning of our wing's name came to mind and reminded me that ultimately Christi was delivered from suffering when she was killed instantly in the car crash. She did not linger for months on life support with a severely battered body. One minute she was in the car with her friend, and the next minute she was in heaven in the presence of her Savior.

It would take me several months to navigate the grief process that rocked my faith in Christ to my very core. To this day, I still do not fully understand the why of her tragic death. Peace finally came to my heart when I realized the why of her death was not important, but rather the HOW she lived while she was here.

We do not know how long our days will be on this earth, but each day we have a choice to make a difference in the lives of those around us. We can also choose to surrender our hearts to Christ and have eternal hope that we will live forever in heaven with HIM. How will you choose to live your life on earth?

Glorious Days

It shall be a glorious day
When we hear our savior say,
Come on home
You no longer have to roam.
On that day we shall
Not be weepy no more
Because we shall be
Before Heaven's door.
When it is opened we shall see
Not a tear or sense any fear
For our Lord will say
Come in here.

Inspiration

Goodbyes can be so difficult, especially when someone has made such a positive impact on our lives. This poem was written after I had to say goodbye to my grandmother who had been a tremendous encouragement to me over the years and spent many of her final years completely paralyzed by illness.

Even when she could only communicate by blinking her eyes, I still felt her love. I miss her greatly, but the thought about her in heaven finally able to walk again and no longer in pain gives me peace. Let these words comfort you as you mourn the loss of those followers of Christ who have gone before you.

Grief

My heart feels sad
From the tears my eyes hurt bad,
It is so hard to say on this earth goodbye
When our loved ones die,
We feel we cannot cope
We struggle to find hope,
There is love ready for us
When we are grieving and want to cuss,
Ask Christ to fill your sad heart
To the top with HIS amazing love that brings a new start.

Inspiration

I have seen many of my friends lose loved ones over the years and wanted to offer comfort while pointing them to the ONE who can heal their sad hearts.

Free

Are you free
Can you clearly see?
Are you blind to a life of peace
That comes from knowing
Christ the Prince of Peace?
Are you a prisoner to your passions
As you strive to live up to the current fashions?
Have you ever tasted love
That doesn't push and shove?
Do you live daily having a joy
That revives your weary soul?
Are you a prisoner to your mind
That keeps you in a desperate and hopeless bind?
Are you free from worry
And the pace of a suicidal hurry?
I once was bound to my mind
In a hopeless state of a desperate bind.
Then I came to the end of my rope
I found an eternal hope
HE touched my soul
And made it whole.
Let Christ set you free
So you can say with me,
I am free and can clearly see!

Inspiration

This poem was composed during my college years before leaving where I grew up in Michigan to attend ORU. I remember meeting students at the community college I was attending who were dealing with severe anxiety and depression, and who wondered whether their life was worth living.

I thought about how Christ had delivered me from these crippling thoughts and given me hope in difficult situations. The words of this poem flowed when I wanted to share words of hope with those I knew who were struggling. May these words provide a path for your freedom from the things holding you back.

Look

Look into the eyes of the ONE
Who can take away your worries that weigh a ton,
Look to the ONE
Who is brighter than the noon day sun,
HE can take away our fears
And wipe away our painful tears,
HE is the friend
That will stick with us until the very end,
HE can take away our worry
When our minds are racing in a frantic hurry,
Look to the King of Kings
Who can take away rejection's sting.

Inspiration

One of the most challenging times we can have is when someone we love faces a difficult path with their health. This poem came to my heart when I sought to have the words for a friend who faced this very challenge. I prayed for God to give me words to brighten his heart and revive hope. May these words do the same for you.

Provider

Our God always provides when we ask HIM to.
HE changes our negative tides.
HE meets our every need
And takes away our greed.
HE assures us he's working on the job
When we are about to sob.
HE IS always right on time
With our each and every dime.
God is the only one who provides in this awesome way
Providing for us each and every day!

Inspiration

Our dreams don't always come fully financed. This poem was penned when I struggled to find a way financially to leave the community college I was attending in Michigan and transfer to Oral Roberts University. There were enough finances to pay for my first semester at ORU, but nothing after. I prayed, seeking God's guidance, and he flooded my heart with peace. I was unsure of my path forward, but trusted HE would be with me along the way. Sometimes, we must take that leap of faith. What is your big dream that is not 100% financed? Will you be bold and go for it?

Hope

When I am bombarded with hopelessness
Can I find lasting happiness?
Does eternal hope exist
When my future is a dark mist?
Is hope truly real
When I'm down to my last meal?
Is there a hope that will last
When the bad reports are cast?
Is there an eternal hope I can cling to
When I'm told there's no hope for you?
Can my hope securely stand
On my mind of shifting sand?
Yes, my hope can do all the above
Because I've placed my hope in God above.
HE brings peace to my troubled heart
Giving me a brand-new start.
HE calms my fearful mind
When the outlook is unkind.
HE gives me the hope of HIS eternal presence
When I feel so hopelessly alone.
HE calms the storms in my life
So I don't have to dwell in strife.
HE speaks life-changing hope
To my mind when I can't cope.
HE fills me up
When I have an empty cup.
My hope is in Christ
Whose presence I can always rest in.
HE will always give me hope
And will never leave me hopeless!

Memories

The poem reflects on a challenging time in college when I found myself lying in the hospital after sustaining a severe inner ear concussion. The concussion had damaged the part of my brain that controlled my balance, vision, and hearing. I struggled with double and, at times, triple vision. I could barely hear and had lost my equilibrium to the point I could no longer walk.

The specialists advised me there was a strong possibility that I would not be able to return to nursing school or ever complete college. They suggested I consider making very different plans for my future. Tears ran down my face as I heard those words and I prayed. I prayed for God to heal my body. I knew he had much larger plans for my life. Those plans did not include my being a prisoner to the physical challenges I was navigating.

The hospital released me with a schedule to follow up with additional doctor's visits and a letter to the dean of nursing at the community college, advising her of my diagnosis. The dean advised she would work with me to make up the missed time in the program if I recovered.

That was the sliver of hope that I needed. I spent the next month praying, standing every day despite the room spinning, and speaking life into my future.

When I returned from my follow-up visit, the reports showed a dramatic transformation over the last month. The results showed a miraculous recovery. I received medical approval to return to school. I returned to campus and shared my great news with the dean of nursing that I was ready to return to the program. She advised I must pay a significant fee to make up for the missed classes and clinics. She further advised, "You will also have a very limited time to make up all the missed hours of the program."

My heart was devastated again, because I did not have the finances, nor could I see how it was possible to make up all those missed hours in such a short timeframe. I went to my favorite place along Lake Huron to pray. I thanked God for healing my body and asked him to guide me. What am I to do next with my life? In those moments of prayer, I thought about my dream to attend ORU, and to learn at a university where they frequently gathered students to go on domestic and international mission trips. The university had clubs filled with medical and nursing students who worked locally providing health care to individuals. I knew what to do next.

I started making phone calls and applied to enroll in the winter semester at ORU, even though it was only a few months away. Miraculously, I was accepted and given enough financial aid to complete that winter semester. So, after being told there could be little hope for a full recovery, I was soon driving to Tulsa, Oklahoma, to start a new life pursuing my bachelor's degree. I was thrilled to be moving towards a career of helping others in their most critical moments.

Each of us has those defining moments in our lives where we are told that the dreams inside of us will not happen. We have a choice to either believe in our hope-filled future or remain frozen in fear. We can believe the reports or roll up our sleeves, believe the impossible is possible, and look to the ONE who can make miracles happen. What will you choose in your defining moment?

Dream

Follow your dreams
Until they flow into golden streams.
Follow your heart
You will know where to start.
Keep the sparkle in your eye
Even when life causes you to cry.
Never lay down and die
And believe the false lies.
March forward with Hope
Trusting God, you're not at the end of your rope.
Dream away
Trusting HE has already made a way.
Pursue your dreams
Knowing you and HE are a team.
Walk through life with a smile
Thanking Christ HE has walked your mile.
Live life as a dreamer
Trusting in the power of your Redeemer.
Open your tired eyes
And don't be shy.
HE holds you in HIS hand
So, in HIS mighty love, you can stand.

Inspiration

This poem was written during my college years before I met my husband. It was during a time when I was navigating difficult days both physically and emotionally in the pursuit of my dreams. I can remember struggling with serious physical issues such as endometriosis, severe hypoglycemic episodes, inner ear concussion, costochondritis, and parasitic infections from multiple travels overseas on mission trips.

I can remember feeling the pain of my family and childhood church friends not understanding the path I was pursuing to follow my dreams and the heartache that caused. Yet, amid all these issues, there was prayer. I prayed for God to please heal my body and broken heart so I could live my dreams. The words of this poem flowed through my pen after one of the many times when God brought peace to my troubled heart during prayer.

Epilogue

Thank you, reader, for joining me in this poetry journey and more. I hope you were encouraged and inspired along the way.

Throughout our journey together I asked key questions and shared lessons to help you discover hope and inspire you to help others.

Here are the questions to help you reflect along your journey:

1. Where can you find beauty in your daily life?

2. How can you bring love's beauty into someone's life today?

3. What things can you express gratitude for in your life?

4. What is your dream? What picture captures that dream? What picture and customized note can you share with a friend to encourage them to pursue their dream?

5. What is your prayer or poem of Thanksgiving?

6. How can we share love during the holiday season?

7. What next step do you want to take in life? What is holding you back?

8. How can you incorporate gratitude into your mindset regarding the place you call home?

9. Where have you traveled to that you never dreamed of seeing?

10. What is one mistake you can forgive yourself for today? To whom can you extend grace today?

11. What stress are you facing today?

12. What is your unique trait? How can you use it to help others?

13. What burden can you give to God in prayer today?

14. Where are you in life's race?

15. What are you living for each day?

16. What burden are you carrying that is keeping you from feeling God's love?

17. What relationship needs mending in your life? What steps can you take to show more love and understanding in that relationship?

18. How can you help others avoid the mistakes you made in your life?

19. Who can you bring a smile to and help feel valued today?

20. What has filled your eyes with tears? Have you given your burdens to God in prayer?

21. How will you choose to live your life on earth?

22. What is your big dream that is not 100% financed? Will you be bold and go for it?

23. We can choose to believe in a hope-filled future or remain frozen in fear during the defining moments of our lives. What will you choose?

Here is a summary of these lessons to empower you to walk in your destiny:

1. Take a few moments to unplug, get outside, slow down, and reflect on what you do have in your life instead of thinking about what you may lack.

2. Do not be afraid to go after skills you thought previously were not for you. Sometimes we just need the right mentor to guide us to successfully accomplishing the task or learn the skills.

3. Choose each day to find beauty and see the miracles in our world.

4. Remember the gift each child's life represents. Find ways to show kindness to the children in your life or that cross your path.

5. It is not about you, but about improving others' lives.

6. Turn what seems like a setback into an opportunity to make a difference in a new way. Look through the eyes of others to understand why they appear to be failing as a leader and see how you can lighten their load for the organization's success.

7. Explaining the WHY and creating unique opportunities for those you lead to experience the WHY ignites excitement inside those you lead to accomplish amazing things.

8. Leadership is a precious gift to be used wisely. It is not for the weak, but rather for those individuals who choose to take the heat so a path can be made to help others shine.

9. Accomplishing amazing things cannot be achieved until we go beyond our comfort zone. We can impact lives positively when we leap out of that comfort zone and focus on meeting needs, placing service before ourselves, and lifting up others.

10. Choose to help others, share hope, and be a friend to all.

11. Find what you DO HAVE and use that to bless others. More will come your way when you share your resources to elevate others.

12. Life is precious; celebrate those around you while they are still alive.

13. God has made a way to mend our broken hearts and replace the pain with HIS amazing love.

14. There are needs around us every day regardless of what city, state, or country we are in at that moment. Each of us has resources and a smile we can share to brighten someone's world. See the needs around you and find ways to help meet them.

15. You are not alone. God can help you win in the most difficult situations.

16. Christ can heal our hearts damaged by hurt and be a friend that sticks closer than a brother. Proverbs 18:24

17. Never lose your faith. Hebrews 11:1

18. Boldly create opportunities to share your talents outside your comfort zone.

19. God loves you and can do miracles in providing you opportunities for beautiful relationships.

20. Christ is ready to offer love, forgiveness, hope, and healing. John 15:13

21. God can help us through our darkest nights. Psalm 42:8

22. Choose freedom. John 8:36

Our next journey together will be one of motivation. I have written hundreds of quotes in my various leadership roles to encourage others to see their potential. I am excited to take you on that journey to help unlock your potential to thrive.

Until our next journey together, I leave you with HOPE.

H ealed from hell and hurt.

O pen eyes to the extraordinary.

P rotected and full of purpose.

E mbrace a new mindset with energy and excellence.

About the Author

Rebecca Strobl is a Certified Protection Professional, Licensed EMT-Intermediate, Health and Safety Institute Instructor, Retired Volunteer Fire Chief, and Youth Advisor, and holds a Bachelor of Science Degree.

She made history as the first female fire chief in the Lake Arrowhead Volunteer Fire Department's and in Cherokee County. She received an official letter of congratulations from a United States Congressman for this historic achievement.

Rebecca's professional background extends beyond emergency services with over two decades of experience in new business development, client retention, employee engagement, training, team building, and motivational speaking. She has captivated audiences worldwide with her ability to weave knowledge, enthusiasm, and humor together in an engaging manner. Each keynote displays her enthusiasm for equipping others to thrive. Her various experiences in corporate America and grassroots volunteerism have honed these skills. Her passion lies in inspiring others to embrace learning and personal growth. Her personal core principles center on being kind, being yourself, and being positive.

She is the founder and president of New Day Education and Motivation, LLC, which equips individuals with the knowledge to confidently make a difference during an emergency and accomplish amazing things professionally and personally. They facilitate launching organizations to the next level of productivity by working with their teams to perform their best work.

Their mission is to inspire others to learn and thrive.

She continues to give back to the community as an advisor for her county's Fire and Emergency Services Explorer Post, where she has mentored young adults ages 14 to 21 since 2012.

She enjoys spending time with her husband, hiking, fishing, traveling, and making others smile.

Meet Rebecca Strobl, EMT-I, CPP

Contact Rebecca about providing your team with an engaging educational experience or to speak at your next event.

rstrobl@newdayeducationandmotivation.com

Follow Rebecca @Rebecca Strobl, CPP, EMT-I on LinkedIn.

Follow Rebecca @Chief Strobl on FaceBook.

Visit **www.newdayinspirationsbooks.com** to order additional copies of *New Day Inspirations: A Poetry Journey* and stay informed of future New Day Inspirations books.